HOURS ON SINAI

Ioanna Tsatsos

Hours on Sinai

Translated from the original Greek by
Jean Demos

Hellenic College Press
Brookline, Massachusetts
1984

Funds toward the publication of this book were provided by the **Archbishop Iakovos Education Fund**.

Orignally published as: *Apo to tetradio mou: Hores tou Sina* by "Estia."

Published by Hellenic College Press
50 Goddard Avenue
Brookline, Massachusetts 02146

Cover design by **Mary C. Vaporis**

Library of Congress Cataloging in Publication Data

Tsatsou, Ioanna.
    Hours on Sinai.

    Translation of: Apo to tetradio mou, hores tou Sina.
    1. Saint Catherine (Monastery: Mount Sinai)
2. Tsatsou, Ioanna. I. Title.
BX387.T7313 1984   248.4'63'09531   84-10877
ISBN 0-917653-009 (pbk.)

HOURS ON SINAI

CONTENTS

TRANSLATOR'S NOTE

TRANSLATOR'S NOTE

The first published work by Ioanna Tsatsos, poet and writer, was in the form of a diary, Φύλλα Κατοχῆς, 1941-1944, later published in English as *The Sword's Fierce Edge.* *Hours on Sinai* is her fifth English publication, and is again in diary form. In between were two prose biographies, of the Byzantine Empress Athenais, and of her brother, George Seferis, also a volume of poems.

The purpose of *Hours on Sinai* is to chronicle a pilgrimage and the time span is only two months. In a sense, however, it is an autobiography. It reveals the activities of a lifetime and the aspects of a personality as fully as a much longer account might do.

In 1975, her husband, Constantine Tsatsos, was elected by the Greek Parliament to serve a five-year term as the first President of the Hellenic Republic. Because of his long participation in the government of Greece, public life was by no means new to Ioanna Tsatsos. To be the First Lady was, however, a large assignment. She was already much involved in good works, both personally and through organizations, already a professional writer, always concerned with learning and study, always active in support of the arts, and unfailingly involved in the fortunes of her country.

From the Presidential Residence, the former Palace on Herodes Attikos, she continued all these concerns, while adding to them a most scrupulous performance of obligations involved in her husband's high office.

But her strongest commitment was to her duty as a Greek Orthodox Christian. And as her diary tells us, the climax was to be a pilgrimage to Saint Catherine's Monastery on Mount Sinai. To do homage to the 1400-year old shrine became her deepest desire.

Readers should understand that the pilgrimage could not take place earlier. While the Peninsula belonged to Israel, a country where, unhappily, Greece does not have diplomatic representation, Ioanna Tsatsos could not go there. When the Camp David agreement in November 1979 changed the boundaries, she could go to Sinai via Egypt. As the date of the diary shows, she lost no time in making her plans. She met some opposition—the President's early objections are noted—but she persevered, and the first section, *Preparation*, indicates how she worked her plans into the complicated pattern of her life.

The poem *Sinai* expresses the essence of a fulfillment for which the diary provides the details.

SINAI

SINAI

Mountains hard in the white light
Rocks deeply furrowed
I spell out your letters in awe
Hermit that I am.
Am I still myself?
I travel on the slender death-boat of the sun
I hear things not heard before.

The glow does not fade
Nor the unapproachable lights
Each cycling flash
Changing shape in the thick silence.

The tree in the middle of the road
Where is it?
Its foliage spreads into a shade
And who can ever explain the greening leaf?

I nest in the dark of earth
Trying to find the life that I had
Before I was born.

I have forgotten my body
But what of thought?
It is scattered by memories
It speaks with the birds.

But how can I nail it
For hours and days and nights
To the great challenge?
Thought is useless.

I set out toward Him in the darkness
I am walking on the sand
My only guide the beat of my heart.
His presence is surely somewhere here
Perhaps I shall touch Him.

Mountains of rock
With your writings,
Solid bastions guarding the monastery,
I wait long and patiently
For the snow to come
So that I can spell out the messages
In the flakes borne by doves
As your signals.

I drank from your well
Then I read in Your mystical writing
The first commandment,
Silence.

I am ready.

A FEW WORDS

A FEW WORDS

Life is memory. What happens is alive because I have it in my mind. If I forget it, it vanishes like the dreams of night.

Absolute sincerity is momentary. What we write is the truth of the hour when we write it. It is the self of that hour. It may be the most durable self; it may be the most fragile, the most fleeting. Our whole life will judge it. Moments weigh us down with an indefinite responsibility. Time takes on a composite meaning. As if the time I live were not mine alone.

I try to be honest. It is easy for me to report events. To convey an emotional truth is difficult. When I reduce it to reason, I feel that other sensations which I have excluded are knocking at the door.

And if I have doubts concerning an idea or about the style, I take scissors to the text. Simplicity is for me an aesthetic necessity.

I hasten to make notes. Time moves faster than our ability to accommodate ourselves to what is happening, faster than our capacity to absorb daily circumstances.

After looking at my recent diaries, I decided that I should publish what concerns the pilgrimage to Sinai. The Monastery of Saint Catherine is a continuation of Byzantium, a part of our living history that has conquered the hostile intervening centuries.

PREPARATION

PREPARATION
1980

New Years Day

I am grateful to God and the Greek people! The year 1979 has ended harmoniously for the good of our country. We have entered into 1980.

On all these anniversaries I turn with tender gratitude to those of the old friends who remain.

But I have no way to speak with myself.

It is easy enough to be decent and just. What is difficult is to give yourself when within you are building an impregnable fortress.

Spirit, acting with complete concentration, requires its solitude, like the moment of love.

10 January 1980 Thursday

Little by little the fuss of the holidays comes to an end. We settle down again.

Much substantial work remains to be done.

If everything goes well, my compelling duty now is my journey to Sinai.

I followed the discussions at Camp David in November 1979, the difficulties of evacuating Sinai and returning it to Egypt.

The authority of Sadat has been recognized. He climbed the Mountain with his wife to give thanks to God.

Now diplomatic obstacles to my journey no longer exist.

For a long time this feeling of great obligation to the Monastery of Saint Catherine has tormented me.

I have felt that Orthodox Greece of today has most urgent reason to continue living in warm solidarity with this never-enslaved Byzantine corner of earth.

I have felt it essential that we should help these Greek monks. For centuries, there in the heart of the desert, through insuperable difficulties, they have kept alive Christian wisdom and the Orthodox tradition while guarding the ancient texts. They have preserved unconsumed that supreme symbol, the Burning Bush. Peoples like the Greeks will grow and prevail only if they consistently fulfill their obligation to history.

That is why I want to go to the Mountain and the Monastery as the Byzantine link in the great chain of Hellenism.

As the time grows shorter, I wake and sleep in persistent thought of the day when I shall actually be there.

How shall I find time on my calendar for this absence? It will not be easy.

The light softens. Thousands of sparrows are winging toward the pine tree near my window. Coming and going they are a breeze in the quiet of sunset. They line up on the branches and look at me steadily. Others, as they come to roost, look like pinecones enriching the tree.

Lusty for life at the beginning of the day, lusty for life at the end. Tranquil and calm at twilight.

It troubles me that I have so little time for my own work. It is the kind of work that demands concentration and discipline. The many daily duties contend with each other. But often the little free time I have proves to be the most fruitful. How long shall I have the inclination and the endurance to work at night? How long shall I be able to discipline expression?

We never reach the limit of our *psyche* by whatever road we travel. So deep is its *logos*, Herakleitos would say:

11 January 1980 Friday

I had an answer from Dr. Casey, the eye-specialist in London. He has studied the X-rays and the records of young Moraitis, the blind boy from Marousi. There is no hope. The nerve is destroyed. Today I expect a visit from his mother. How shall I tell her? This kind of sorrow absorbs me completely. On the 15th of August last year, I saw this handsome eight-year old boy lying at the shrine of the Virgin in Marousi.

When we see someone powerless on the edge of disaster, our sense of responsibility is a nightmare. What happens then? We plunge into silence because in that hour any expression in deed or art is futile.

I am tortured, so I take refuge in unworthy thoughts to find a little relief. I say to myself that I am not that other person. He has his own world, his own defence in sorrow or joy. But my imagination has assumed that his world is exactly like mine. Does my imagination sometimes exceed the reality? Or can it perhaps never reach it?

The clouds are low. It may snow this evening. The cypress trees shrivel; motionless, they speak of patience, of the acceptance of fate.

"Compassion is the crucifixion of the soul – and whoever can, let him put his soul on the cross."

13 January 1980 Sunday

Yesterday we had the reception for the journalists. It was pleasant. Not like the usual receptions. The guests were lively, knowledgeable because they are exposed to so many sources of information, full of ideas, quarrels, jokes, always ready to make friends with immediacy and ease. Away from political pressure, in the general mood of friendship based on common interests, I understand them better. Every day they are confronted with columns of blank paper, and they must fill them, whether or not they feel inclined to do so. Hard work.

The evening's atmosphere was one of intellectual relaxation, and they talked with unique spontaneity.

A friend said to me, "Poetry as a political weapon is never good poetry. A party line is always antipoetic."

"But perhaps the truly great poet is able to surmount the the weakness of personal feeling in whatever form," was my reply. I was thinking of Dante. Led on by the poem's essential beauty, we forget about his hates and antagonisms; we forget that most of the damned were Dante's enemies.

14 January 1980 Monday

I have appointments almost all morning. Friends, people with grievances, ambassadors' wives, some coming to say goodby, others who have just arrived. They are usually charming, interesting women, and in a lively way they reveal their worlds to me. I enjoy listening to them, traveling with them.

The depth of winter. Clouds low. The wind whistling. In the garden, the trees stand shrunken, like disheveled women.

I spoke with my husband about my trip to Sinai.

"This is not the right moment," he said. "Wait a little."

"Every postponement is failure," I answered, "for every tomorrow is more full than today."

16 January 1980 Wednesday

Before me I have an inspired picture. It is a view of the Monastery (Pierre du Mans, Paris, 1554). There it sits as if in the hand of God. Mountains, like great fingers, are protecting it. How could it be otherwise? Through fourteen centuries of world-ferment, of invasions and attacks by barbarians, pillage and massacre have left this corner of the earth unchanged. On every free evening I am studying its history.

> In the early years of Christianity, many anchorites took refuge on this mountain where God had walked.

They led their hermit lives in its caves. There is a tradition that Saint Helen built a church near the well where Moses met Jethro's daughter. About 400 A.D., Aitheria, traveling as a pilgrim from Galatia, recorded that she found there many scattered sketes, and also, near the Bush, a church where the ascetics were worshipping.

Later in the fifth century, barbarians invaded Sinai and slaughtered the hermits. Fear and terror reigned in the area.

Emissaries came to the Royal City and begged the authorities to safeguard their sojourn in the desert. Theodora had died in 548, and that is when, according to Prokopios, Justinian decided to build 'the strongest possible fortress' as a protection for the anchorites, and also a basilica dedicated to the Virgin of the Burning Bush. This was about 557 A. D.

From then on the Holy Monastery was firmly established in God's hand, a response to man's faith and his thirst for eternal love.

17 January 1980 Thursday

I write random ideas on scraps of paper in preparation for a book which, perhaps, I shall never write. Journeys in the realm of history, worked over in dreams, and always charged with beauty.

The spirit knows nothing of inaction and repose.

Thoughts and impressions at every split second. They come and are lost, and only the fixed idea and the deed constitute the outer man.

I read in the diary of a political refugee:

It was my spirit they were sentencing. They took away my eyeglasses, my pen and paper. Ideas come and go, one after another, and some are lost and come back in another connection. One idea may remain constant, others disappear, often the best ones. I search and I cannot find them. That is why I cannot sleep, always looking for those I have lost, and fearful lest I lose the next one, the one I believe to be unique. I don't care about bread. I want only paper and pencil. Without them, how can I bring order into the chaos of my mind?

18 January 1980 Friday

Today is a great day. The beginning of the realization of my plan. I have asked our protocol officer, Mr. Vakalopoulos, to inform the Prime Minister of my desire to go to Sinai.

19 January 1980 Saturday

I have been working with Neokli Koutouzi. He is translating *Chronos*[1] into French. This work is deeply refreshing. Koutouzi is a true scholar in both prose and poetry. He is engaged in a great undertaking: the presentation and criticism of all the Greek authors in forty volumes.

By the hour we discuss the significance of every word and turn of phrase, first in one language and then in the other, each one with various shades of meaning. The difficulties are often unforeseen. Then he comes forth with brilliant solutions in keeping with the poetic meaning. He himself is a poet, and quite indifferent to fame and glory.

The mind creates friendship nourished by a shared ethos.

20 January 1980 Sunday

To the Museum of Natural History in Kifissia. What unimaginable variety and beauty in all these creatures of earth and sea! There was a two-winged shell. What had it locked there in its closed heart? Its silence wiser, more impressive perhaps, than all our books.

21 January 1980 Monday

There is fighting in Afghanistan. Hunger and cold and death are nothing in the face of the passion for freedom. How long can it hold out? The leaders take refuge in phrases and protests without effect.

Words! Words! Our bitter experience for so many years in occupied Cyprus.

Every day we have crimes all over the world, so enormous that the one swallows up the other. Finally they cancel each other out, and all are forgotten. And this is a grave matter. To coexist comfortably with injustice is unacceptably callous. Every day ends with accounts of the most unbearable, the most horrendous events.

What is happening? How much of all this is the mad need for action and self-projection, and how much is in the service of some ideal?

We must be deeply aware of our weakness. What of the child? To what kind of world are we committing him? What resources for self-defence do we offer him? How shall we fight greed and deception while the television is giving us details of a perfect crime with the most up-to-date methods? Are we so irresponsible?

Lately I have been studying the Bible. Its poetry is refreshing.

> Now Moses kept the flock of Jethro, his father-in-law ... and he led the flock to the backside of the desert, and came to the mountain of God, even to Horeb. And the angel of the Lord appeared to him in a flame of fire out of the midst of a bush; and he looked, and behold, the bush burned with fire and was consumed...And God called on him out of the midst of the bush, and said: 'Moses, Moses!' And he said, 'Here am I.' And God said, 'Draw not nigh hither; put off the shoes from thy feet, for the place whereon thou standest is holy ground. Moreover, I am the God of thy father...'

And Moses said unto God, 'Behold when I come
unto the children of Israel, and say unto them, the
God of your fathers hath sent me to you; and they
shall say unto me, What is his name? What shall
I say unto them?' And God said unto Moses, 'I AM
THAT I AM,' and he said, 'thou shalt say to the
children of Israel, I AM hath sent me to you.'

22 January 1980 Tuesday

Jacques Lacarrière passed by. How he loves Greece, and
how well he knows it! That is why his books are so dear to us.

We had some discussion about Olympia. A picture comes
to mind: Apollo in the center, a god, with one calm move-
ment holding off the evil. The Lapith woman, bent over, in
all her strength and beauty, supreme in the grace of unwilling
submission.[2]

Round about, the tourists in greens and reds, lifeless figures beside the living marbles.

24 January 1980 Thursday

The New Year appeal, a book offered as a gift for the holidays, had a great success this year. Today those who had ben-
efited from it came to say thank you. The book circulated
as never before. The supply in the stores was exhausted, also
in the kiosks. A good beginning.

25 January 1980 Friday

Little by little the chain unwinds. The Prime Minister
makes no objection to my trip to Sinai. I spoke about it with
Ambassador Phryda. I had known him in New York when I
was working at the United Nations, a responsible man with
wisdom and imagination. He has sent to Cairo the request
that they take the necessary steps for me to visit the Mountain.

Patience.

Hope may bring us what we did not dare to hope for.

26 January 1980 Saturday

A long talk with the envoy from Sinai, Father Nektarios. He told me about all the shadows, all the needs, all the fears that confront the Monastery. During the latest war between the Hebrews and the Egyptians this piece of earth was bathed in blood.

The Monastery needs our concern. Only its tradition sustains it, this vital Byzantine Orthodoxy, a chalice that the monks hold in their hands.

It is absolutely right that I should go to them. If only my visit will encourage a few believers, both secular clergy and monks, to man the great Monastery fully, as it once was.

27 January 1980 Sunday

Sunday. A breathing spell. To my books. To concentrate for a while on ideas. What a comfort.

> The powers of the earth, subjects of the one God in whom we all believe, conferred their favor on the Monastery. The prophet Mohamet, in his famous testament, the Achtinamé, promised his goodwill and protection to the monks of St. Catherine's Monastery, and all of Islam respected the prophet's wish.
>
> Later, in the tenth century, the legend of the veneration of St. Catherine brought a new brilliance to Sinai. Angels appeared to carry her precious body to the highest peak of the mountain rising beside her monastery! There the monks received it, and now it is in the sanctuary of the basilica. The church is dedicated in her name.
>
> In his calendar, Symeon the Translator, famous hagiographer of the tenth century, writes:
>
> St. Catherine was martyred in Alexandria under Maximos. She was a pious woman, young in age, very beautiful in appearance, of royal blood, and learned in

wisdom acquired both from us and from abroad...
At the very moment of her demise, angels appeared,
and after laying out her sacred body, they brought
it to Mount Sinai.

I stretched out in the great heart of the night. Its pulse
was my pillow. A white light became a beam in the darkness—
my guide. When its warm, fertile breath caressed me, I came
into being. Reluctant or eager, I was caught in its cycle.

At work or asleep, I am always pursued by some poem.
This one is a Christmas poem, the Virgin Mother in Her glory
and Her joy. I cannot rest until I achieve its final form. She
has lost her ten-year old son, and where does she find Him?
In the temple. Only on Christmas is the Babe her own. Before
me I have five versions, but none satisfies me. Now I have
written something else, and perhaps it will serve:
"But neither the evil ones—
nor the Spirit,
not even Your soul
could take You away from me then,
could separate You from me.
I was Your world,
Not the Spirit, not even Your soul. . ."
There is a love we carry within us even when memory
fails.
More at peace, I fell asleep. Tomorrow I could look at it
again.

28 January 1980 Monday

Today the exhibit of Greek books. I look at them, turn
their pages, one after another. How many of them say anything? How many of them have anything to say? I lived again
the hard hours of the writer, when the idea is taking form.
Now, to rest a little, I pick up the *Bucolics* of Virgil. Tre-
mendous powers of intuition, of visualization, of poetry.
Dante did well to choose him as guide through the other

world, all the way to the gates of Paradise. There Virgil delivered Dante to Beatrice.

> And vanquishing me with a smile of bliss
> She spoke to me: 'Turn now and listen anew!
> Not only in my eyes is Paradise.'
>
> *Paradiso* 18:19-21

Seventy years before the birth of Christ, the Cumaean Sibyl had prophesied it. In the surge of his inspiration, Virgil would also foretell the coming of Jesus. Beyond the evils of the time, the poet sensed the depth of his spirit:

> This child shall have the gift of divine life and shall rule a world to which his father's virtues have brought peace...the earth shall be freed from the shame of fear...the serpent shall disappear, and the poisonous plant with all its deceits. *Eclogue 4*

The poet's vision transcends time, and his longing to see humanity redeemed and happy emerges in celestial pictures of the future alive with the truth of his poetry.

Poor Virgil! He feared the censorship of his work by Augustus, and was tortured by the persecution of his friend, the poet Cornelius Gallus. Nor could he write of him as he would have wished to write.

All his sorrow is expressed in the line: "The earth shall be freed from the shame of fear."

Fear in the eyes of a human being—what is more abhorrent, unbearable!

28 January 1980 Monday evening

Bitter cold.

I look at the newspapers. In the New Democracy Party, the battle over the succession. When Parliament elects Karamanlis President of the Republic, who will be Prime Minister? Averof or Rallis? How will the election take place?[3]

And this is all premature. Why discuss it now? Why must we constantly breathe uncertainty?

Again my husband said to me: "Your trip to Egypt is most untimely at this point." He may not be wrong. Every day we fight this climate of the provisional. And what moment is "timely"? Who knows about tomorrow? Our only hope is today.

In any discussion we are influenced by the wisdom and the intelligence of our *vis-à-vis*, but we must also pay attention to his complexes. These subconsciously influence his judgments.

29 January 1980 Tuesday

Is there any hope of justice?

At the Islamic Conference in Islamabad, thirty-five ministers of Foreign Affairs, together with Iran, accused the USSR by name for the attack on Afghanistan. Perhaps this is a sign of more effective solidarity among these coreligionists. Who knows? United in their indignation, these peoples might exert some influence.

Our ambassador to Cairo, John Iannakakis, brought me the news. My visit has been announced to the authorities in Egypt. They are expecting me. The dates are fixed, 28 February to 4 March. We shall have official hospitality. They offer us the palace El-Tehera as our residence. And most important of all, we are to have an army plane to take us to the Mountain to stay as long as we wish.

They ask who will accompany me so that they may prepare the program.

There will be Academician Constantine Trypanis, the literary scholar. His lively interest in old manuscripts and editions, and his knowledge and feeling for the Byzantine ikons will make his presence a fruitful one. His Oxford English, as well as his discretion, will be helpful in all the official contacts.

Then there will be Professor Jean Demos, widow of

Raphael Demos, many years professor of Greek philsophy at Harvard University. She is an Orthodox Christian of deep commitment, sensitive to all beautiful things.

There will also be Tassia Kappou, my secretary, and Thomas Makris, the Palace butler, indispensable on every expedition. As always there will be the two security officers who never fail to accompany us.

I have asked our ambassador to thank the Egyptian authorities warmly, and to emphasize that this journey of mine is a pilgrimage to the Orthodox Monastery of St. Catherine.

Is it possible? Shall I really be starting in a month? Within that month will some obstacle appear? Natural disaster? Illness? The end of Tito who is even now wrestling with death? No. Nothing must happen this month. Later.

The closed rooms are choking me. I must go down to the garden. The tangerines are at their peak. Let me breathe deeply, very deeply.

Tomorrow we are expecting the wife of the President of France who comes to inaugurate the exhibition of Impressionist paintings in our National Picture Gallery.

30 January 1980 Wednesday

Today is loaded with obligations.

At eleven o'clock to the airport to meet Anne Aymone Giscard d'Estaing. Hers is a reserved personality, but her deep feelings reveal themselves in times of stress. I sensed this when we made our official trip to Paris and went to the Monument of the French Resistance at Mount Valerian.

I had been asked why I would wish to visit with Mme. Giscard on our free morning. At that moment I heard again the secret radio to which we had recourse during the Occupation: "This is Free France." All the pictures of their tragedy came to my mind. We had been comrades-in-arms, and I asked leave to deposit at the grave of their dead a lykithos containing soil from the tomb of Marathon.

That morning there were just the two of us. Her father had died in exile; he was not one of the million who returned.

And how many others did not return! As we drew near, the flags of the resistance battalions dipped to greet us. In that historic moment, overpowered with a sense of gratitude and obligation, it was a comfort to have her near me.

Here in Athens today, her program was continuous, almost without intermission. From the airport directly to Aghia Paraskevi to dedicate the French-Greek lyceum. Only at noon did she have a little time to herself. She liked the Maximos Mansion,[4] and took notice of the pictures by Ghika and Moralis. In the evening there was the inauguration of the Impressionist exhibition. Color and light. She spoke with appreciation, but with moderation. This calm atmosphere prevailed also at the dinner given in her honor that evening at the Presidential Residence.

Tomorrow she leaves for Rhodes.

31 January 1980 Thursday

Today I went back to the Museum to look quietly at the Impressionists. I asked Basil Goulandris to go with me. He lives in Paris, loves painting, and has studied all aspects of art, contemporary and traditional.

It was a marvelous morning. What a joy to give yourself at leisure to a work of art and to feel proud of being a human being!

> "Car c'est vraiment Seigneur le meilleur
> temoinage
> Que nous puissons donner de notre dignité."
> *Baudelaire*

Tonight solitude did not produce the customary refuge. It was a sleepless tranquility. For two days I had not touched a book.

> The worship of Saint Catherine was conveyed to the West by the monk Symeon. About 1025 A.D. he carried a few relics of the Saint from Sinai to Rouen. From then on the Roman Catholics have venerated

her memory with profound respect.

Not influenced by the Schism, the Popes made rich gifts to the Monastery, and Orthodox monks on pilgrimage were always supplied with recommendations. Ships flying the Monastery's flag were respected.

In Crete the Doges of Venice recognized the property of the Monastery and accorded it special privileges. At Chania the Sinaiatic monks had founded the Theological School. Patriarchs and other important clerics had been students there. In difficult years, the tributary of Sinai assisted during the absence of the Orthodox bishop.

And what invaluable services the Monastery offered to Orthodoxy during the harsh years of enslavement. In that wild period when tyranny ruled, the monks of Sinai, led by divinely inspired abbots, kept coming and patiently transmitting Christ's teachings. Both to the criminal masters and to their victims, they conveyed tenderness.

The great Sultan Souliman renewed the privileges conferred on the Monastery by the Achtinamé. At that time the Bishop of Sinai was the wise and universally respected Eugenios. From early times, the abbots of the Monastery, beginning with St. John of the Ladder, were men of great learning and sanctity.

2 February 1980 Saturday

Yesterday I visited the Refuge at Aghia Paraskevi. These girls are not really orphans, but they have no parents. For various reasons, their homes have disintegrated. Fathers and mothers perhaps disturbed, perhaps with other interests. But here the children seem to be robust and happy. There is light and love in their eyes, at every moment the expectation of some unlikely magic, and the readiness for an open embrace. Young cypresses, waiting for cool water to make them burgeon.

Today to the Home for the Elderly at St. John Karea. In the dim eyes of these old people, another kind of expectation, neutral, without sorrow, without joy, with acceptance.

We concern ourselves with children to prepare them for life. The old people stand weakly on the threshold of death. Theirs is a quiet plea for help in pain.

3 February 1980 Sunday

How quickly events grow stale for the general public. It has lost interest in the courage of the people of Afghanistan, in the plight of the diplomatic hostages in Teheran. They speak of all this as they do of their evening meal.

At noon I had my first direct contact with the Monastery: I met the abbot of St. Catherine's, Father Damianos. His full title is Archbishop of Sinai, Faran, and Raitho. Faran and Raitho are tributaries of the Monastery there on the peninsula of Sinai. Two high mountains meet at the walls of the Monastery. On one peak, the Lord delivered the Ten Commandments to Moses. On the other were found the relics of St. Catherine.

The abbot was able to give me an overall picture of the monastic life of the Mountain. He explained their great need for our support and cooperation. Our talk was constructive. I listened. I asked questions, but there remains much for me to learn.

Today I have stopped swinging from one concern to another. This obligation to the Monastery takes precedence from now on.

4 February 1980 Monday

The protocol office in Cairo has organized all the details. The program has gone to print.

This evening I felt as if I were already there.

I read: Most of the ikons on Sinai are marvelously well-preserved by reason of the very dry climate. One can imagine that they were painted only yesterday.

I slept. I was a very small pebble at a point which was to become a beach. Within the darkness, patiently, fearfully, I heard the waters and the whistling winds. Mountains were piling up, higher and higher, cataracts were rushing down.

I waited, waited, stirred by hope as the universe was being created.

I wakened. But the warmth of hope did not leave me. And I wanted it never to leave me, so deeply did I feel that I was participating in the Mystical Creation. The day wore on, and moment by moment I felt that a priceless power was leaving me. And I wanted to hold onto it, in whatever form, by whatever means, so as to be saved from my unbearable diminution, my transformation into nothing.

How one's idea of time changes! When I was small, I scorned it. At one period I was choked by a melancholy which I could not throw off. Our house was as if it were in mourning. My father and my brothers were abroad. I accumulated morphine from my sick mother's medicines so that I would have available the means to die. When disaster actually came, I was ashamed of those thoughts. My elders were asking support of me, still a mere child.

Now time has changed into a still more severe interlocutor. "Give to me so that I may give to you what I take from you."

The moment makes heavy demands. They must be met. Otherwise, the daily transformation becomes nothing.

5 February 1980 Tuesday

The planning of future events tires me more than the events themselves. And they are becoming more and more significant. I must go on this pilgrimage free of responsibility, but the work of the staff must proceed while I am absent. Nothing, however, must hold me back.

Today began well. I had a visit from the Bishop of Komotini. We have been working together over the building of their cathedral church. The problems are endless, and they are serious. The state will give no further funds. We have appealed to the engineer, Axiotis, and to Constantine Trypanis, who, as Minister of Culture, had laid the cornerstone of the church. Also to the Under-Minister, Gerasimos Apostolatos. With intelligence and imagination he has found many ways to help.

Some time ago we ordered the reredos from a well-known wood-carver at Metsovo. It is a gift to the church from our friend, Dolly Goulandri. Now it was ready. There remained the iconography. It was our common decision that it should be achieved by making copies of great ikons. We had already an agreement with the Byzantine Museum. We went there, and with the help of the director, Paul Lazaridis, we spent hours making our choices. We wanted simple ikons in which the figures of the saints were of good size. Only so would the expressions on their faces be well perceived by worshipers at the back of the church. When we confronted Christ and the Virgin as depicted by Tzanes, we were overjoyed. Even now I feel that joy. It was as if I myself had painted them. We persisted in our search and found the other saints and the wonderful Annunciation from Patmos.

We placed the order which will be paid for by donations.

6 February 1980 Wednesday

The banks are on strike. Also the personnel of the telephone company. How is democracy to make progress with all these strikes?

Last night we received the judicial community. Our guests were well-known citizens of high moral standing. They felt comfortable with each other.

One friend said to me: "Life in the provinces is difficult when you occupy a judicial post. Our every act, every decision, is examined and judged in the cafes. Adaptation is a daily struggle. Little by little we get used to it. Every solution involves compromise between merits and demerits. What cannot be compromised is freedom. But are we any longer free? So enslaved by others? And finally by ourselves?

Night. Back to my monastery.

> In Egypt in the twelfth century a protective order by the Sultans renewed the special privileges of the Monastery. It safeguarded the vast property from raids, even the holdings in Palestine, Syria, Crete and Cyprus.
>
> Much later Napoleon, and, after him, General Kleber, Commander of the French Army in Egypt, were concerned to rebuild carefully Justinian's walls which had been destroyed by earthquake.

7 February 1980 Thursday

Patrick Hillery, President of the Irish Free State, is visiting Athens. Last night he was our guest at dinner.

"From the ancients we learn precision of speech," he said to me.

"But how talented you Irish are," I continued. "Quite rightly you take plenty of Nobel prizes. And so many of you are Philhellenes! I'm sure you know that Oscar Wilde wrote from prison to Frank Harris—"I am a Greek who made a mistake when he chose his period." And we spoke about Yeats whom both of us greatly admire.

> "I am of Ireland
> and the Holy Land of Ireland," I added.

From London President Hillery sent me a beautiful edition of Yeats with this sensitive inscription: "May it be, in the word of Thucydides, a possession forever."

All foreigners who share our classical learning are in a sense Greeks. So said Isocrates. And there are many. I have sensed this over the years.

Fires everywhere. The tragic situation in Rhodesia. The dangerous diplomatic game, often beyond human ability. Peace, indeed the life of the whole world, dependent on a wise or a senseless human thought, on a wise or a senseless reaction on the part of a leader—it is a nightmare. Glory must be a small reward for those who assume responsibility for the fate of the world.

8 February 1980 Friday

Light snow. It will thicken tonight. The fireplace is lighted. A poor little sparrow hits the windowpane.

In the early evening, we went to the French Archaeological Institute. Pierre Amandry described the year's accomplishments to us. Beloved Greece! So many treasures underground! Philippi, Argos, Crete. The island of Thasos, with inexhaustible antiquities and much natural beauty. Nature embraces history in a rare synthesis. At Artemision they have found the Propylaia of the Sanctuary.[5]
Nature, art! Does death exist?
I looked around me. Many old friends, so aged and indifferent. What about me?

9 February 1980 Saturday
General Rogers makes a new proposal to bring Greece strongly into NATO. He will confer with General Grazio in Brussels.

About martyred Cyprus, only silence.

A coalition government is ruling Yugoslavia. Tito's life hangs by a thread. Will he live for twenty days more?
When we give our hearts, a well of suffering pours forth.

10 February 1980 Sunday

I went for a walk on Hymettos in the light fog, as in a green cloud.

Time without activity is something precious, sacred. Time in its essence, without anxiety, without haste.

The quality of this day was almost perfect. I was lost in the shelter of its filtered light. Our Lady must have been resting somewhere there under a tree.

The earth is a graveyard, dry branches, withered leaves, friends who have left, friends who are leaving every day.

Nature a quiet affirmation of life and of death.

Mother Earth, you embrace us and give us your love. Let us also be givers.

I continue with my reading of the Bible. Pure poetry, full of substance! This newborn imagination embraces all things and speaks confortably with its Creator because it feels Him close by, using the unique form of expression, poetry.

God made the world, Man made the word.

What marvels in an acre of earth! Thousands of green shapes, playing with the sun, swinging in the breeze. The tangerine trees heavy with fruit, and whatever the heart can hold.

What marvels in two lines of verse:

"Thou hast enlarged me when I was in distress . . ." (Psalm 4.2).

Pain and patience and hope and trust in the Creator's work, and what is there more? Whatever the heart can hold!

And further in the same Psalm:

"Lift up the light of Thy countenance upon us . . ."

The highest possible triumph, and what is there more?

It is a great responsibility to be honest and unsophisti-
cated in our thinking about Man and about God.

11 February 1980 Monday

An old woman from New Ionia came to see me. Thrown
over her shoulders was a richly embroidered silk shawl. She
walked with difficulty. I beckoned her to be seated.

She looked at me tenderly.

"What a beautiful shawl!" I said to her.

"I was wearing it, and that is how it was saved from the
fire. From then on every day was a gift to me from God."

Thomas brought her coffee. She looked carefully at the
silver tray.

"You know, my child, I had two such trays. The fire
took them too, with whatever else I loved."[6]

The tears of the old are different. They do not flow.
They remain fixed in the pupil of the eye, and make the
eyes shine, shine with the awareness of resignation.

"Les yeux sont des puits faits d'un million de larmes,
Des creusets qu' un métal refroidi pailleta . . .

Baudelaire

That resignation. I know it well. I, too, have walked that
narrow daily road, those sad, nightmarish paths. And I, too,
have rolled down that precipice.

12 February 1980 Tuesday

Television. Speeches in parliament. Rhetoric. The words
actually mean nothing, but the crowd follows the pompous
rhetoric in the vain hope of discovering some significance in
this weighty discourse.

The word is watered down, it disintegrates. Now comes
the writer, the poet if you will, and he must save the word
because he needs it, because without it he is crippled. He
must bring it back to life in its first innocence. He tries to
grasp implications which will throw a new light on it. He

himself enters into the symbol in search of a fresh expression.

Letters and verses and books from many young people are an embarrassment to me. They ask my opinion. They are waiting for the miraculous word, and how I wish I could speak it. I understand them. We are all longing for the word of encouragement. But why must they be in such a hurry? Think of the poems Seferis tore up until he was twenty-eight. As for myself, I was writing from girlhood, but I did not decide to publish until I was forty years old. Perhaps it would be helpful to the young if I could make them understand what endless inner patience art requires. Let them keep writing because now and then ideas of some value will come forth. Let them put these writings in a drawer. Then let them study. A time of revelation will come, through events or through reading, to bring them face to face with their own wisdom as they derive it from the tragic depth of life or from intuitive intelligence. Then they may be stepping on firm ground. They themselves will know when this happens. And if it does not happen, let them try something else which they will do better.

13 February 1980 Wednesday

What are we going to do about crime? Since the beginning of the year, twelve assassinations in Italy. That is to say that every three days someone is murdered. Today in the heart of Rome, at the Law School crowded with students, another murder.

I ask myself what identity remains for the man who kills an unarmed human being in cold blood. What is his relation to himself? Even if he gains money and power and escapes prison? How can he pursue his life freely when he has taken the life of another?

"And righteousness shall be the girdle of his loins."
Isaiah 11.5

And where is righteousness?

14 February 1980 Thursday

There came to my hands an old letter from the last Basque to be executed by Franco. The brave fellow wrote to his sister: "You who have years of life ahead of you . . ."

That phrase took on a strange dimension.

The day is calm—then we chance to read something. It presents a picture, wakens a painful memory, and suddenly the world of ancient drama lives again in us.

In a dream my brother, Angelos,[7] appears. The first time since his death. He is thin, but handsome with his gentle smile as in the old days. We were happy at being together. I threw my arms around him and kissed him, then woke with the heavy sense of separation. Memories, longings, fermenting during the labors of daily life, had seemed forgotten, but they remained there deep within me, and their red, red blood glistened in the darkness of sleep. It hurts me that they are buried so far away, Father in Paris, Angelos in Monterey. If their graves were near, we could caress them from time to time. Even a single green leaf would relieve the tormenting sense of our debt.

18 February 1980 Monday

I am to see Jean Demos at 11:30. She is translating my poems into English. We agree that words of Anglo-Saxon origin should be used whenever possible. Words with Latin roots sometimes convey the feeling of our Katharevousa, somewhat artificial, pretentious.

Every expression has taken on a different shade of meaning over the centuries. I study the translations of my poems trying to find in them my inner rhythm.

20 February 1980 Wednesday

Every day we read the news with astonishment, and in

the end we are surprised at nothing. Five members of the International Council of the UN will examine the Shah's record. A strange procedure. Who is on trial? The United States? The Shah? How much forbearance is required just to live—how much silence!

And how much compromise with the claims of valor and integrity!

This morning Alexander Philon came to see me. He is leaving to be Consul General in Constantinople. We talked about what we both value most in the depth of our hearts. I asked myself: would I like to be in his shoes? I think not. But when I feel the breeze of Ionia, it raises familiar worlds of dreams and imagination. There is much within us which we have not actually experienced! Much that comes to us from the flow of memories, subconscious, but enduring!

The God of Christ was based on Old Testament traditions. He loved mankind. He did not wish to destroy him.

I have not sent my latest book of poems, *Duty*, to anyone. I prefer not to distribute my books while my husband is President. Nevertheless, we have a real need for a response to whatever we write.

21 February 1980 Thursday

I am quite indisposed. My head aches unbearably. I am reading the newspapers in bed.

We have broken off our dialogue about our entrance into NATO.

I have just spoken on the telephone with Manolis Andronikos.[8] I want to put him in touch with Stelios Triantis. Triantis is an artist of great sensitivity, working at the Archaeological Museum. All our guests have marveled at his copies of the murals from Santorini. He would certainly make a successful copy of the Persephone from Vergina, an important piece of classical painting recently made available to us. Andronikos knows Triantis well and agrees to help

him. This will make it possible for us to show our guests at
the Maximos Mansion the unbroken history of our painting,
ancient and contemporary.

A news flash from Tito. His last political act: a message
wishing for the peace of the world, sent to Brezhnev and
Carter. As I think of Tito, I remember Milovan Djilas' words
about him.

> Often Tito was both the helmsman and the wind.
> Born of the Revolution, he was taught in the Soviet
> Union that institutions and power are more important
> than ideals. But Tito learned that institutions collapse
> if they are not cemented by some ideal. In politics
> where everything contributes to a single aim, Tito was
> a rational, not a dogmatic leader, and he made use of
> ideals.

22 February 1980 Friday

We are drawing near. Five days yet to go. That is not long,
but it seems ages when we want something with this almost
painful intensity.

I am frightened because from now on, a problem will not
merely postpone our pilgrimage; it will cancel it.

23 February 1980 Saturday

What an irony! Someone is laughing up his sleeve. We
stupid 'immortals' are afraid of hindrances from outside,
and here it is I who have fallen into bed with a temperature
of thirty-nine degrees.

"Doctor, help me as much as you can, but temperature or
not, we are leaving on Thursday."

I have seldom fought with such intensity of spirit the
events of every moment.

24 February 1980 Sunday

The same. Temperature and pain all through my body.

This form of gripe reminds me of the old dengue fever.

25 February 1980 Monday

The temperature continues. Double antibiotics. After today I shall not take my temperature. For those two final days let it be what it will.

26 February 1980 Tuesday

The newspapers full of contradictions, and chaos in the headlines. "The election of the President is taking place in an atmosphere of political crisis."

I am sorry to be leaving my husband at such an uncertain moment.

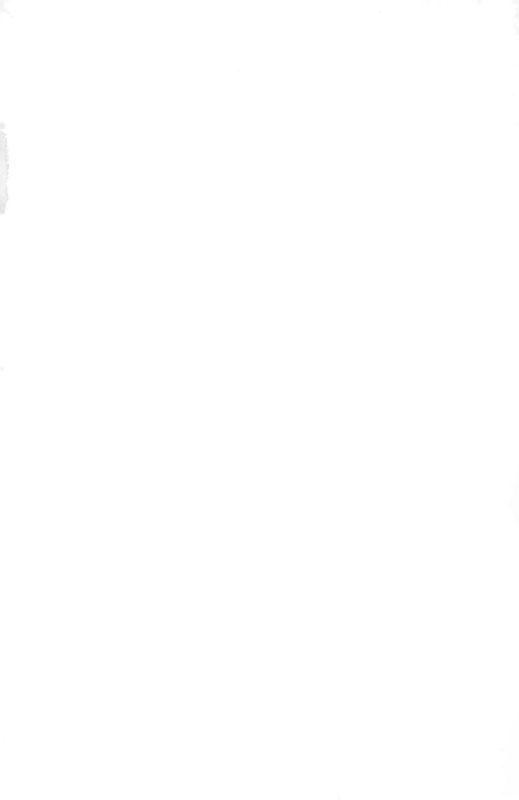

GOD'S GRACE

GOD'S GRACE

28 February 1980 Thursday

"All things were made by Him, and without Him nothing was made that was made." This pilgrimage will take place because He willed it.

All these words strive to say something of importance. I sense this.

Every hour God opens His arms and scatters abroad His miracles. Whoever comes to understand this, whoever opens his soul to receive them, let him take the road of preparation to be worthy to receive them.

One's view of man changes. It takes on clarity and perspective. And reason too takes on perspective. What remains is a broad understanding of what is happening.

But this low fever makes me weak and ineffective. Help me, Christ, to raise up this flesh which is sometimes so heavy, so heavy!

Woman of little faith, you do not deserve what God is giving you!

We are on our way.

Cairo   29 February 1980   Friday

Where am I? Still sunk in my bed, I hear the voice of the Muezzin. Through the open window comes the first light, the songs of strange birds. Now I remember.

We reached Cairo late in the evening yesterday. Jehan El-Sadat was waiting for us at the airport, beautiful, friendly, gracious. I presented our ambassador and the members of our embassy. And she, in turn, presented the members of the committee of honor.

Mme. Sadat accompanied us here to Heliopolis to the Palace of El-Tahera where we were established. It is an elegant residence with precious pictures and furnishings, and marvelous rugs. It is surrounded by a large park. Not far away is the Coptic Church of the Virgin. It is considered a miraculous shrine because in her flight from Herod, the Virgin took refuge here with the Christ Child.

Thoughts of tomorrow occupied me until I retired.

In the famous museum, treasures of art and wealth. The gold of Tutankamon, the art of the Pharaohs. Century after century of history and worldly vanity.

Near the Pyramid of Cheops, well-guarded in an enclosed area constructed for the purpose, is the ship that carried the souls of the dead to the sun. Long and slender, light as air, fashioned with rare skill. The builder knew that, in their final quest for perfection, these souls were weightless. The vessel was found buried deep at the base of the pyramids. On it Cheops was to make his journey to the sun.

Dinner that evening at the Sadat residence in Guizéh. There I made the acquaintance of the family. Before us flowed the Nile with all the magic of its history and the splendor of today's civilization.

1 March 1980 Saturday

Now away from the commotion and the diversity of the city, we move toward Thy summit.

How much time, how much of mind and heart have gone into this day. Now it is here, a day free from what until today had seemed the most important, the truest, the most precious things of life. Free even from the sense of deep obligation to the Byzantine Greek monastery which in recent years had become an *idée fixe*. Free also from the longing to enjoy and to live with the old ikons and manuscripts.

All these vanish, effaced by the overwhelming brilliance of the moment.

"I AM THAT I AM."

From the abyss of our destruction, we are to approach

the imperishable.

> "They shall not hurt nor destroy in all My holy mountain: for the earth shall be full of the knowledge of the Lord, as the waters cover the sea."
>
> Isaiah 11.9

How much man needs God if he is to compensate for his nothingness! His presence completely fills the open heart, as it fills all nature.

His call is addressed to all mankind. And the answer to this call is the pull we feel within us toward the Divine Power.

This sense of being drawn to God, whether as a quiet parallel to daily work, or within the frame of religious observance, or in the tragic struggle to enter more deeply into the cycle of the Creator, is one more proof of His existence.

We were escorted by the First Secretary for Foreign Affairs, by the military governor of the Mountain, Ezza Wahba and his wife, and by the chief of protocol of the Presidency, Nasser El-Ansari and his wife.

The biblical landscape unrolled before our eyes. The pilots arranged to seat me near them so that I could better observe our passage. There was the line of the Suez Canal, and soon the Red Sea. Then we went into the mountains, jostling each other in irregular relief, and seeming to be full of significant signs. I could hardly wait to see them more closely, so strong was the impression that great messages were imprinted on their crags.

Now the landing at the airport of St. Catherine. At last we are in her kingdom, and soon we are on the road to her Monastery. See, there are the historic walls. Only a few steps more.

At the entrance, a huge Greek flag, one with the heavens.

The sound of the wooden semandron and the chanting of the monks. The Archbishop Damianos is there in his golden robes to receive us.

Carved on the lintel of the great wooden doors, an inscription in large round letters. I managed to read it:

Through this gate of the Lord
let the righteous enter
I AM THAT I AM

At that moment I believed that Orthodoxy past and present was showing me the way. I heard the Doxology, and my heart was beating as if to break. My tears flowed. Here was never-enslaved Byzantium, here was the continuity of the nation throughout time.

Life is this fire within us, moment by moment binding us to Thee, through art, through history, through nature. And we hasten forward to overtake it.

We venerated the relics of St. Catherine, and the Archbishop gave each one of us her holy ring.

Each monk contributes something of inestimable value to the work of the Monastery. Father Sophronios tirelessly oversees everything as guardian and keeper of the keys. Father Paul is the steward in charge of the household. The scholar, Father Demetrios, is the librarian. With what touching concern, with what sense of mission, he keeps in order the unique manuscripts and parchments of the Sinaiatic Codex. But what can one man accomplish alone with these thousands of treasures? There is a great need for assistance, for a supporting staff.

Finally, we are taken to the Chapel of the Virgin beside the Burning Bush, but I cannot bring myself to enter at this moment. I let the rest go in to make their devotions, and they do so, shoeless, reverent. But the presence of so many persons has altered the quality of my emotion. I must wait a little.

The chapel is dedicated to the Annunciation, symbol of the divine Fire that embodied Christ. The ikon to the left of the Holy Table shows the Virgin with Jesus in her arms, and it is as if they are surrounded by the Burning Bush. On the right, Moses, in an attitude of adoration. Centuries have passed. The Bush continues to bloom outside the Chapel.

Alone now. On my knees. Feet bare. The silence deepens. Deeper, deeper, in His mute presence. An endless moment. A drop of faith. An ocean.

The holy silence is broken by footsteps. I hear the Archbishop's voice:

"The Nunnery of Faran is some distance away. There is the desert to be crossed and the road is not good. We should leave immediately."

I put on my shoes and went out.

"Let us go now so as to experience the desert in both light and darkness."

Only a few came with us.

We leave the lone tree and the well of Jethro behind us, and move on through the low hills with their dark caverns here and there. Surely this is where the hermits would have sought refuge.

The oasis of Faran is referred to in Genesis:

> And God heard the voice of the lad, and the angel of the Lord called to Hagar out of heaven. . . 'Fear not, Hagar, but take the lad and hold him by the hand and I will make from him a great nation' . . . and he dwelt in the desert of Faran."
>
> Genesis 21.17

Faran was the first Christian center on the Peninsula, dating from the fourth century. It was also the first seat of the Bishop of Sinai, Faran, and Raitho.

As we drew near, the landscape became more gentle, more mild, more familiar. There was a breeze from the oasis. A few date trees, a few palms. The water a life-bearing wave. Likewise, in their defiance of time, the ruins.

It was like an evening in spring.

The nine nuns of the convent received us with open arms. Their talent as housekeepers shone in every corner. The Bishop celebrated vespers in the little chapel of the prophet Moses.

They treated us most generously, showing their joy in every possible way. Rarely do they have a visitor in this corner of the desert. We found it hard to take leave of them.

Night had fallen when we set out for the return. The moon, almost full, was partly hidden, and gave form to the clouds, a face, a swallow. Now the hills rose black in the half-darkened dome. 'Angels and powers,' centuries of prayer and holiness, were continuing their summons through the night. "The spirit of God moved . . ."

Surrending myself to this atmosphere of worship, I felt deeply my unworthiness. Doubt seized me. God neither appeared, nor did he hide Himself. He mattered.

Lord, give me a sign. Am I worthy to step on this, Thy chosen land?

Let my humility be deep. Thou art my only glory. Today as I entered Justinian's church, Orthodoxy in all its splendor wakened in me great pride, but it was pride on behalf of all Greeks.

I opened my heart like a book, and read there all my trespasses. Lord, Thou knowest that I hate no one, nor can I hate, nor judge, nor be envious. But there are many I do not love. Calculating and hypocritical, they seem to me ugly. My soul cannot breathe in their presence.

"Love thy neighbor." How difficult that commandment. And always the question, who is my neighbor?

Another heavy obligation. However hard I try, I cannot look after all those who need help. Some leave me with a persistent remorse, and I keep going back to them.

And how many other omissions, unjust reactions, and vanities revolve threateningly around me! Often failure to act is more unkind than an evil action.

And then, my God, how much I need a little time for myself. I often feel mutilated as I give away my hours. Something within me demands solitude.

But my heaviest sin comes in my hours of doubt when I

feel that my prayer is being lost in the void. Then I am utter-
ly lost. I am trapped by logic, by the concerns of the day,
by the intoxication of activity. I do not allow myself to be
drawn to Thy mystery as I am now in this holy moment.

And there comes to my mind the words of Ionesco one
evening in Athens:

> When I was young in Roumania, I was swept toward
> God as on a great wave. I went to Father Alexander
> to confess. Unassuming as a child, but with the as-
> surance of one who has lived long, he said to me: 'I
> am not a confessor. However, did you steal? That
> doesn't interest me.'
> 'Have you been incestuous? That hardly more.'
> 'Just tell me one thing—tell me, do you believe?'

Help me, Christ, because I love Thee. I reach toward Thee
as do the poplar trees, as do the high mountains. The love
Thou hast poured into Thy creation, firm, impenetrable—
that Love is also in me. All is a wasteland when I lose Thee.
Whoever doubts Thee, tortures me. My own doubt is my
deepest concern. I fight it, and I conquer it. Thy sacrifice
is a lamp which lights the shadows. The mystery which en-
velops Thee is my torment.

Thou who givest serenity to the humble, Thou who
dost trample death and dost offer us the infinity of time,
help me.

And my woe, drop by drop, that too must be reckoned.
Open wide my soul toward Thee.

I was fleeing, fleeing, and as the distance from the life of
the world increased, I drew nearer to the eternal essence.

I felt that the great Cross on the summit of the Mountain
was protecting the whole desert. From the sketes I heard
prayers, winging lightly on the breeze.

Lord, I am waiting for Thee. Bend over me in my agony
of heart. Give me a sign.

This prayer was heard. It was not lost on the wind.

And Jesus answered, "someone has touched me, for
I perceive that virtue is gone out of me."

Luke 8. 46

A short time before, at Faran, it had been summer. They
had set our tables out of doors. Now the clouds were gathering and changing their shapes. Suddenly, quite unexpectedly,
it began to snow and the snowfall became heavier and heavier.
The flakes opened out as they brushed the headlights of our
car and created the most unlikely patterns. It was as if there
were a breach in the dome and through the opening were
coming white sea gulls.

Behind me I heard Archbishop Damianos crying out with
enthusiasm: "Baraka, baraka! A blessing! You have brought
us a blessing! It almost never snows in the desert."

Such dazzlement! I wanted to gather the storm, indeed
the whole world, into my arms. Here in utter solitude was a
ladder from heaven to earth. Was I a creature newborn? The
light of the desert enveloped my soul.

The snow grew thicker. Visibility was less and less. The
road was difficult to follow. We reached the monastery late.
Exhausted, we climbed to our cells to sleep. Tomorrow the
great liturgy would be celebrated. We would all receive communion.

How did that night ever pass! Out of consideration, they
had given me the largest cell in the guesthouse. It was on a
corner with three windows looking toward the Mountain.
Through their cracks the snow penetrated the room. I heard
it whistling round me. I felt it in my freezing breath. I
tied my head in a woolen shawl, wrapped myself in whatever might give me some protection, and tried to read so
as not to think of my freezing body. Time was as if
nailed to the spot. My watch had not stopped, but it showed
the same time. I opened the Gospel which I found beside my
bed. It fell open at the passage in Matthew:

"Enter ye in at the straight gate."
Matthew 7.13

The monk who had left it here seemed to have read that passage often. I read aloud so as to involve all my senses in my effort to understand its meaning. The wind continued to blow madly. Snowflakes struck the windowpanes. I took a few steps up and down the room so as to move about a little. Click! The electric generator had blown out. Complete darkness. The straight gate was becoming even more narrow.

I sat down and waited motionless. The cold took possession of me. It rose from my feet to my whole body. I waited, waited. What time could it have been?

Was that whistle from the storm? No, it was a more familiar sound, a human sound. The semandron. Now a ray of light was piercing the darkness. It was growing light. I prepared myself and opened my door. My eyes were dazzled by the whiteness and the splendor. The mountains, the Monastery, completely wrapped in snow. The stairs, horizontal columns of ice. I sensed that this gift was worth all that it had cost to achieve it. I was beginning to identify with the Mountain.

"Earth and Heaven dance together..."

This ancient Byzantine church, guarded against time and storm, for centuries had resounded with the undeniable truth of worship. For two thousand years, Christ, Your blood in our blood, Your Word in our hearts.

All is devotion, reverence. Infinite peace. In my stall I grew accustomed to the half-light as I gave myself over to the Psalms of Matins. The chandeliers, the marble columns, the ikons of Our Lady and the Saints were all things I seemed to have known in another life.

I looked around at my companions. Jean Demos had been the first to arrive in the church. In spite of a painful knee, she had come down the icy steps alone, carefully, but without fear. She had scarcely reached her

stall when a shadow passed before her in the dim light.
It was a monk, spreading a thick rug so that her feet
should not be cold on the stone floor.

And there was Constantine Trypanis, unshakable in his
faith in the Greek idea. There, too, Tassia Kappou, faithful
secretary; tireless Thomas, the officers of security, Holidis
and Demetriou—all would receive communion. I was glad
I had them with me so that they, too, could share this
experience of Orthodox faith.

An act of love has no end. It is an offspring of the
soul that goes on and generates life.

The archepiscopal Liturgy of the Byzantine emperors
required three and one-half hours. Justinian and Theodora
are named among those to whom it is dedicated. Byzantium
lives on in its splendor. Who would dare speak of servitude,
of the fall of Constantinople?

The climax of those hours. The mystical ecstasy of
Holy Communion. All of us received. In the early years
of Christianity the gathering of the faithful must have been
much like this.

2 March 1980 Sunday

Following the Liturgy, the Archbishop asked us all to
go to the reception room. My body was functioning better
now, but I had some other unexpected sensations. I thought
that those around me were all very wise. Perhaps they were
not. Nor did it matter. What did matter was this special
dimension which I wanted at all costs to maintain. What
mattered was this hope rising in our hearts.

"Now I know in part, but when that which is perfect is
come, then that which is in part shall be done away."
1 Corinthians 13. 9-10

Christ dying, took with Him human pain. The heavens,
opening to receive Him, received also the sobbing gasp of

the earth!

There in the reception hall, the Archbishop officially received me into membership in the Order of Saint Catherine, addressing me with a few words to which I responded briefly. Each member of the party was given a medal, commemorating in both Greek and Arabic, the historic date, November 1979. Then Brother Paul treated us each to a glass of cognac and a *loukoum*.

The snow and the storm continued and our departure was uncertain. Now the time was ours.

I went back to the empty church, deserted now, even the sanctuary. I wanted to examine quietly the ancient mosaic of the Transfiguration there in the apse. Its brilliance was staggering. Christ clad in gold and silver appearing in all His glory.

The verse from Matthew came to mind!

"His face did shine as the sun,
and His raiment was white as the light."
Matthew 17.2

The two prophets, Moses on the one side, Elias on the other. Kneeling, bewildered, the disciples, John and James. At Christ's feet, Peter.

I marveled at the technique. The abstraction and the symmetry emphasized its spirituality. The work is almost intact although it belongs to the time of Justinian.

Then I went back to the Burning Bush. Its attraction was irresistible. There time no longer exists.

We had scattered. I wanted very much to see the old refectory. In monasteries, these tables convey a two-fold meaning: the holiness of the Spirit through the blessing of the daily bread.

The overhead arch is of Gothic shape, and an expressive mural of the sixteenth century depicts the hospitality of

Abraham. The entire hall has a medieval feeling.

Waiting for me in the sitting room, I found Constantine Trypanis with Father Sophronios. Together we went to the gallery of paintings; there Professor Soteriou had selected some of the best ikons for our examination. Then on to certain locked treasuries where countless other portable ikons are stored.

My impressions were so many, so intense, that even persistent effort fails to recall them as I would wish. But one sixth-century crucifixion stays with me: Christ does not bow His head. He is not yet dead upon the Cross. He looks straight at us, motionless, with those large eyes of the East. He is giving Himself for us. To the very end He is acting in full consciousness of His inestimable sacrifice.

There were the wax-encaustic ikons of the early centuries, reminding me of the words of the modern iconographer, Fotis Kontoglou: "A thousand years were needed for the Virgin to move her little finger."

Other ikons of the eighth and ninth centuries are in the Eastern style with their own frugality and charm. Having survived the battle with the iconoclasts, they follow their own even way. But in the years of the Komneni, we begin to see evidence of the Renaissance. Vivid colors now, symmetrical composition. Faces expressing expectation. An unusual *Ascension of Christ* on a gold background made a special impression on us. The Virgin is in the center with an angel on either side, in the background sparse little bushes. Also a remarkable menologue in gold and read and blue. The Monastery should certainly have an atelier to maintain the paintings and decipher the codices. There is a close connection between the technique of the illuminated manuscripts and the technique of the ikons. A number of the Sinaiatic monks were painters: Palladas, Pangratios, Ieremias.

How true, how deep is our faith, we ourselves do not know. Except for some moments of Divine Grace, faith and love, fluid as they are, require daily exercise. But this much is certain: throughout the centuries, while the holy hermits, withdrawn from the world, were painting the sufferings of Christ, they were sharing in His martyrdom. And we sense their compassion, their sympathy, in the ikons produced by their genius.

Quite by chance, there comes to mind now a unique mural, rescued and preserved in an abandoned chapel on Aegina. Who was the exceptional artist so able to iden- tify with Jesus, that he depicted himself on his knees in dialogue with the instrument of martyrdom, the Cross? What sorrow, what power to accept was shown in the in- finite depth of His expression!

How well I remember the poet, Sikelianos, quietly contemplating it, and later writing of it in a sonnet:

> In his eyes, the last coherent thought
> Thickens into a cloud thicker than dumb silence
> So that my mind confronting it cannot distinguish
> The immeasurable Passion from the painted work.

How can one comprehend and appreciate so many masterpieces in so short a time? The entire place is a museum. I've said nothing of Damaskinos and Tzanes and Kornaros whose work we know well. The Monastery has always been in touch with the Cretan School of Chania.

With Constantine Trypanis and Jean Demos, I squeezed into the library, the famous Library of Sinai. In recent times one whole side of the Monastery was rebuilt, leaving the ancient walls intact. In a large room they have estab- lished the library. It is well-organized on two levels and is equipped with all the new means of protection against fire.

Brother Demetrios was our guide. He is a monk with a de-
gree in philology from the University of Thessalonike, and he
is absolutely devoted to the old editions. He works with zeal,
often far into the night, to preserve them, to clothe them in
muslin so that they should not fall apart, and to arrange
them in chronological order. The director of our National
Library, Nikolopoulos, has shown him some of the tech-
niques.

By a very narrow staircase we went up to the second level.
Manuscripts–priceless–all around us. Seven thousand ancient texts. Everything we touched was a revelation of art, of
living history. I held in my hands a work of Gregory the The-
ologian from the twelfth century with remarkable miniatures
in blue and gold. There was also the biography of Saint John
of the Ladder, famous throughout the Christian world. He
was the Abbot of the Monastery in 570 A.D., and was called
"of the Ladder" because of his well-known treatise on the
ascetic life, *The Ladder to Paradise.* He maintains that the
suppression of all passion is the highest of the Christian vir-
tues. A contemporary fragment of his text was recently dis-
covered. How many works of art have been inspired by Saint
John's Ladder! This may be seen in the famous murals with
their indelible colors in the medieval monasteries of Roumania.

Saint Catherine's Library has more than three thousand
codices, many of them decorated with unique miniatures.
Some were produced here in this library, others in Constantinople, gifts from the emperors. The bond with the Royal
Capital was close. In one corner, guarded and preserved with
special care, are some parchment pages from the Sinaiatic
Codex of the Holy Scriptures, all that now remains to the
Monastery although it once possessed the entire file. These
few were found in 1975 in a pile of rubble under the Chapel
of St. George. The roof had fallen in and buried them. There
are many other rare editions and manuscripts, even some
commentaries on the Codex Justinianus.

What a rare education a sojourn at the Monastery can
provide!

From ancient times until today, the Greeks are like plane trees lining a long avenue that leads us to philosophy, to poetry, and finally to holiness.

(Sudden news brought me cheer. Our plane would not be able to take off. The storm was continuing. This unforeseen gift of time here among such texts was most valuable.)

Wherever we turned, new discoveries. Here was Anastasios, he too an abbot of the Monastery, later Patriarch of Antioch, a famous religious poet as well.

Ancient fragments of the Iliad with line-by-line translation. Fragments too from Aristotle.

Each new text transported us to its epoch, and all the testimonies of the past became a glorious present. I was moved as I looked at Brother Demetrios, so modest, so simple.

"He is carrying our history on his shoulders." I thought to myself, and I whispered gratefully to him, "Brother Demetrios, how can we help you?"

"Send us monks, even for short periods of time. Send us Orthodox Christians who believe, who love their history, who know the value of a fine book."

Father Ambrose was calling us to the noon meal. Would it be fasting food? Would we freeze? Were we short of sleep? In point of fact, that hot bean soup with a dash of oil was something unforgettable.

In serenity of silence, our daily bread.

I went back alone to the church. Quietly I examined again every detail. The twelve granite columns. The crosses carved on the capitals. The double-arched Byzantine windows.

At my ease I studied the other mosaics that decorate the apse of the sanctuary. The Virgin, John the Baptist, the Angels, created by Byzantine artists, older perhaps than those of Ravenna.

In the sanctuary the first sarcophagus of St. Catherine, in marble, also the other one, worked in heavy silver, a gift of the Tzars.

Then once more I took refuge in the Chapel of the Burning Bush.

Now it was time for me to rejoin the monks and my friends. They were happy to tell me that the wind had abated and that we would be able to leave that evening. For a moment my heart was heavy. I longed to see it all again, but it was for me only to give thanks to God and to my fellow human-beings for all that I had been given.

I took leave of the Archbishop and thanked him, as I did separately each monk. I felt the deepest gratitude to those few holy men who are carrying on their shoulders such a tradition. Each had become an old friend, so intense were the moments I had lived with them.

The Bedouins looked at me with their sad eyes, sorry to see us leaving. Quiet people, expressing themselves in the simplest movements, they could not live without the Monastery. For a long time they have been imbued with its atmosphere, its serenity. They go about their work with devotion, without haste. The friendliness of our smiles, the warmth of our appreciation, brought life to their impassive faces.

As before, the captain of the plane courteously offered a seat beside the pilots. Again the landscape unrolled before me. Sensing my great interest, the pilot made several turns above the Monastery. Our wings were like those of an eagle hovering over the nest. Still fascinated by the grooved mountain and the Monastery nesting in its bosom, I could not speak. How could I ever return to day-to-day life? I managed to ask if we could make one more pass over this spot of earth. We almost brushed the cliffs. I longed to be Siblyl, able to read those mystic writings to which I was now so close.

The mystery of this land is deep. Its spirit rises to dizzy heights. It was not by chance that the Lord chose to touch this piece of earth with His voice.

We plunged into darkness. As night came on, the storm gained power. Wind and wet snow. The landing was difficult. Around me I saw that people were nervous, uneasy. Vicky Ezzat came and sat beside me with affectionate concern. I smiled at her confidently. I knew that she shared my thoughts, from the calm of her spirit, from the light in her eyes.

I thanked the Minister of Foreign Affairs who had accompanied us. I expressed the warmest gratitude to the pilots and the rest of the airline personnel. What they contributed to our journey was beyond price.

The snow-clad Sphinx received us with some surprise.

In our lovely warm residence, they immediately gave us hot tea. Everyone expressed sympathy for the hardship we had undergone—snow is so rare in Egypt. They could not imagine that we would risk travel in such a storm. But the officers and the others who had served us now understood very well the enormous importance of the Monastery of St. Catherine in the eyes of the Greeks. Since, by chance, I was well-known at the time, my every act, however small, was noted and it carried weight. Certainly every Egyptian, official or unofficial, was aware that the Monastery is truly Greek.

The effort had been exhausting. After the intense cold and the lack of sleep, a soft warm bed.

But that night, it was I who did not wish to sleep. I did not want to lose a single inch of the course we had followed. In that hour, faith was clear like the ocean in the first rays of the sun. I believed, believed passionately. As if I had seen Jesus Himself, in peace and truth. And I *knew*. Not through logic, that miserable vessel sailing on the wild sea of nothingness. I knew with an understanding that included whatever truly exists, what appears and does not appear, what is born and what dies, all that embraces God's secret righteousness. Because He knows how vast, how diverse is the human soul, and He believes in it.

LANDING

LANDING

3 March 1980 Monday

Still some obligations. We visited the church of the Patriarch, dedicated to Saint Nicholas, and made our devotions in the traditional way. We were received by the Patriarch's representative, Ioachim. In this land, so many Greek roots, old and recent; they are ours, of our blood, though few of them know their fatherland.

This evening an official dinner with Ambassador Iannakakis. The Embassy building reminds one of the glorious old days of Hellenism. And the atmosphere was warm and cordial.

All the guests were Greeks, and each had something special to contribute. Amalia Nikolaidis, head of the Press Bureau, was George Seferis' assistant during the Occupation. They worked closely together through the serious psychological situations and problems of those days. The military attaché discussed our landing yesterday. He had considered it dangerous, the fog thick and visibility zero.

4 March 1980 Tuesday

At 7 a.m. Jehan El-Sadat was at El-Tahera. She was carrying her briefcase. After taking her leave of us, she was to go to the University to teach. We had seen some university classes being held in the Mosque. The students sit cross-legged on the floor around the professor listening attentively while he instructs them from his chair.

We left immediately for the airport.

The formalities of farewell were like those of our arrival. I warmly thanked the Minister of Social Welfare, Amal

Osman, who had so often been beside me. She is a woman of few words, serious, with faith in her work; she was certain that by the end of 1980 every Egyptian would be assured of his pension. Can we believe that this will be achieved? But why not? She has proved that her love for the people and her devotion to her work are unshakable.

Why not indeed? Because in every era, including our own, there are those who with hard labor and honest effort long to help mankind.

I looked again at the friendly faces of our embassy staff. Such a lively feeling for their country in these border-guards.

4 March 1980 Tuesday

Athens again. Again we must stitch the fabric of our worldly life on the other side. Again Greek newspapers, monotonous, the same. Again discussion in a vacuum. Will the Prime Minister become President of the Republic? This is the big question.

The morrow is good, and it is right to look forward and make plans. But what happens today? Today is our historic responsibility, vital and demanding, according to the strength at each man's disposal. Postponement is a waste of time.

Abroad it is the same again. Tito dying every day without dying. The hostages in Teheran, and the fruitless efforts of the American commission. The great drama of Afghanistan.

NOTES

NOTES

1. Χρόνος, poems by Ioanna Tsatsos, in Greek 1980, in French 1981.

2. The famous marbles of the West Pediment of the Temple of Zeus at Olympia, depicting the fight between the Centaurs and the Lapiths, and dominated by the figure of Apollo.

3. The President of the Hellenic Republic is nonpartisan and elected by Parliament. The Prime Minister is automatically the leader of the party holding the majority. Karamanlis' election to the Presidency would require the New Democracy party to choose a new leader. Averof and Rallis would be the two chief contenders.

4. Maximos Mansion is the guesthouse for official visitors of the Presidency.

5. All references in this paragraph are to archaeological enterprises under the French Institute.

6. This episode concerns the Smyrna disaster of 1922.

7. Angelos Seferiadis, younger brother of George Seferis and also a poet, died in California in 1950 while teaching in the Army Language School at Monterey.

8. Manolis Andronikos, professor of Archaeology at the University of Thessalonike, and excavator of Vergina.